Confessions of a Millennial

Go-Getter

By: Chisolu Isiadinso & co-authors

Copyright Notice

For information on bulk orders or to have Chisolu Isiadinso speak at your event please contact: chisolu@chitheprototype.com

Table of Contents

Chapter 1

Revolving Doors

By: Chisolu Isiadinso

Life is like a revolving door, you walk through one door of opportunities and old opportunities are left behind. Walt Disney once said, *"Around here, however, we don't look backwards for very long. We keep moving forward, opening up new doors and doing new things, because we're curious...and curiosity keeps leading us down new paths."*

Curiosity has played a major role in my success as an entrepreneur. I never believe in the impossible because I always felt that the possibilities create success and positive mindsets trigger achievement. When I look back on my life from my childhood to today, I realize that anything I put my mind towards was achieved through positivity and faith. The reason I am so ambitious is because I have seen dreams come to life with a vision, plan, proper mindset, and execution. I am not here to sell you any false hope; however, if you have faith, believe in your dreams, and never quit working towards them, then the doors will always open in your favor. During this chapter, read my story and know that dreams do come true if you believe in yourself first.

My story begins as a curious college student looking for an opportunity to lead the student body and serve as a role model. Some say that college days are the best days of their lives. I agree because college was golden for me and I had everything I could want. Southern University A &M College in Baton Rouge, Louisiana provided me with an opportunity to be myself, believe in the possibilities, and chase my dreams. At Southern University is where I served as the campus queen, matriculated in Political Science, graduated magna cum laude, pledged Delta Sigma Theta sorority, and fell in love with the passion to make my own rules and be the person who I was called to be.

Before studying at Southern University, I was a tomboy that wasn't into pageantry. I didn't imagine that I would be crowned campus queen! While in college I also had the opportunity to travel outside of the country and see so many possibilities that with the right plan and taking action, I could experience.

With everything going so well for me in school, I thought I had everything figured out. After graduation I received a reality check. After spending four years in college doing the right thing, serving as a campus ambassador, making top-notch grades and having a social life, I still did not have a job in my field of study upon graduating. In addition, after scoring three points below the desired score for the law school admittance exam, I felt as though my dream of being a lawyer had been crushed.

The summer following graduation I landed a job as a receptionist for a local attorney, who was a lawyer for a friend of the family. I didn't stay two weeks at the office before I turned in my notice. To my surprise, I hated working at the law office; it just was not for me. The lawyer was not personable and he always seemed so unhappy and tired. In addition, his paralegal was not willing to train me on the basics of the job. She seemed very threatened and I felt there was no way she would want to see me get anywhere near the lawyer.

To date, that position has been one of the worst job experiences! I realized how much I did not like reviewing cases, filing, etc. Although it had been my lifelong goal to become an attorney, this was the time that I had to determine my true passion for the legal field was not what I thought it would be.

After leaving the law office the best job I could find was at the local Toyota Dealership as a Sales Consultant. This job was a great learning experience for it revealed my passions for helping people, selling myself, selling the product and marketing strategies. It brought me back to my childhood memories of when I'd bring candy to school to sell to other students during gym and recess. I was reminded that using my charm to sell to customers that needed a product brought me joy.

Eventually I was recognized as a top sales consultant in a sales meeting. At that moment I realized that I was working in this position for a reason. I stopped feeling vulnerable about not getting into law school and about not working in the field for which I had a college degree. I realized that all the sales and business skills I was obtaining from this position, I could utilize them to my benefit. I used this as an opportunity to learn as much as I could.

After selling cars for a few months I enrolled in a graduate program and obtained my Master's degree in Business Administration. Deciding to return to school allowed me to walk into a new door of opportunities that would change my life for the better.

While I was enrolled in the MBA program I took advantage of every resource offered to students in business. I participated in the annual Opportunity Funding Corporation, which was a program designed to promote entrepreneurship. This event changed my life because it provided me with an insight on selling products, services, and myself on the next level.

I tried to take that concept and apply it to selling hair extensions, waist trainers, and concierge services. I made decent money, but I was not happy selling items for which I really did not have much interest. Selling those items were cool, but I felt like they didn't fit where I was in my life. For example, when I sold waist trainers I had to meet strangers all around the city of Baton Rouge in order to fulfill their orders; it wasn't safe. In addition I was buying my products from a third‑party vendor, so I could never make the profit I wanted unless I could find the resources and money to connect with a direct vendor in Columbia. Being a student I did not have the money to travel to Columbia, so that was not feasible for me.

It seemed like entrepreneurship was for me, but I knew that I was missing something. I was putting my trust into other people to make money for me. I knew that the way I was doing things would have to change. For a few months, I stepped out of entrepreneurship and focused on paid internships in the business field. I was excited because I was making money. Earning $23 an hour working at an oil and gas corporate office felt like a lot of money and it was consistent. This was the most money I had ever made in my life and it kept me focused on going to work so I could receive that check. Trust me that got old quickly.

I got tired of my internship because there was no real training, my managers just piled plenty of papers on my desk and I sat in a cubicle doing eight hours of research.

In addition, the work was not interesting and my manager pushed me off on another manager in a different department. I always thought that Corporate America would be appealing and that receiving an entry- level position would help me move up the corporate ladder. It was not at all what I imagined.

As I worked for 5 days a week making $23 an hour my brother, Alvin, had found success in his exterior cleaning business. My brother was self-taught in this industry. He researched and watched plenty of YouTube videos. He left his $60,000 a year job and grossed six figures in his first year of his new business. He was taking trips, enjoying life and best of all- he did not have a boss dictating his every move. I knew that something had to change in my life. I knew that I had to close some doors behind me and decide to walk into new doors of opportunities.

Sometimes in life we enter the doors or exit them based on our current circumstances. Soon thereafter my brother suggested that I open a painting business. Based on the number of inquiries he received for a painter after he cleaned the exterior of the homes, he felt as tough it would be a viable business. He told me that for the entire year that he had been in business that he had been referring his customers to other people.

Initially I was quite sceptical. I did not know much about the paint industry nor did I really know where to start. I used my time at my job to research online and learn as much as I could. Every chance I got, I was searching online for information on how to start the business, materials needed to begin the job, and how to generate leads. In addition, I enrolled in free courses offered by SCORE and SBA. As graduation was approaching and I wasn't seeing any possibilities of the manager from my internship hiring me as a supply chain planner at the plant, I put my time and energy into starting my own company. I did, however, have a job offer from Wal-Mart. I was not excited about that position as it was an hour commute to and from work.

I remember the week leading to gradation as if it were yesterday. I had been saving money from my job and wanted to purchase a vehicle for my new mobile painting business. The day after graduation I was up early and went to the state's surplus auction in search of a vehicle. After hours of disappointment and people bidding higher on the vehicles that I wanted, I finally bid and won the auction for a 1996 Dodge Ram Van 1500. The auctioneer started the bid off at $500 and even though I knew nothing about bidding I just raised my number every time he spoke. When the bid got to $1200, I remember the auctioneer pointing to me and saying, "sold to the pretty young lady on the first row." With only about $1,000 in my savings after the purchase, I left with my Dodge van and a mission to win.

As the summer of 2015 approached, I began my career at Wal-Mart as a Warehouse Manager and travelled the one- hour to and from Baton Rouge to Opelousas, Louisianaa every day. Although I was working a full-time job, that never stopped me from building my business. For six weeks straight, I attended a workshop designed to help minority small business owners gain jobs with the state and government. At this free program I learned the business side of the construction industry. I also was offered the opportunity to apply for a grant offered by the university.

After working full time as a manager in Opelousas, Louisiana and attending the workshop twice a week, I was determined to get my business in order before the end of 2015. I realized on my journey that most people want to be their own boss, but they are not willing to sacrifice things to get there. For one year I sacrificed money, sleep, and time to get my business off of the ground.

After the program was over I had information and resources to start my business. The program offered monetary awards to the organizations that pitched their business idea and I was amongst that group. I won $5,000 in a pitch completion. In addition, I received another $5,000 in matching funds in form of a grant from the economics department at Southern University.

The money I received allowed me to pay for my professional website, flyers, vehicle wrap, business cards, and equipment to start my painting business. Through persistence, dedication and motivation I saw my business growing in front of my eyes through the seeds I planted by going to a few events around town to learn more information on how to succeed in my business. Doors were opening for me rapidly and I actually had no time to pause.

At this point I had everything that I needed for my business except customers and painters. Working an hour away from home became even more difficult as the holiday season was approaching. It was mandatory that each employee must work extra days during this peak season. My job was now becoming a roadblock in my goal of entrepreneurship.

My solution was to find another job in the meantime. After looking online for a job near home I ran across a job posting for a manager trainee at the Sherwin Williams Paint Store, which was 1 mile away from my house. Time, knowledge, and field experience were the three things that popped into my head. My goal was to apply at Sherwin-Williams, learn how to attract customers, learn how to articulate painting services and products to customers, and learn on the job while being paid.

After applying for the job, I was offered the opportunity to begin within two weeks. Although I took a $10,000 pay cut, the hands on experience I would receive made it all worth it. The experience that I could gain from this position would save me the thousands of dollars I'd otherwise have to pay a consultant. While there were plenty of advantages there were also disadvantages to my new job. My manager was rude and I felt as though she had her favorite employees; I was not one of them.

However, I pushed forward with the end goal in mind. Even though I went without training for a few weeks, I took it upon myself to walk in the store and learn more about the products that painters use daily on the job. I also learned quickly about the sheens, textures, and coatings needed when painting, staining and varnishing. If you are not in the paint industry I am sure that all seems foreign to you. Initially it was foreign to me as well. I had to learn as much as I could for soon the regional manager would determine in which store I would be placed as the manager; it could be anywhere in the Louisiana region.

After working for two months I was forced to put my two weeks' notice in because I was selected to move to Alexandria, Louisiana (2 hours away from home) and serve as the new assistant manager. I quickly declined that job because the goal was to build my business. I always have a backup. Just two weeks before learning I had to transfer, I was offered a job at a local warehouse in Port Allen, Louisiana as the Third Shift Warehouse Supervisor. I left Sherwin-Williams with manuals on every product, contact information for contractors and a new job waiting for me paying more money. I am sure that now you are thinking I like to move jobs a lot, but honestly I see it as using the cards I was dealt. It was so crazy how things worked out in every situation. It was like I was meant to succeed in this new business venture. I didn't complain about anything because my mind was so focused on winning.

I worked at my new job by night and ran my new painting business in the day. My first painting job started in November of 2015 and it was horrible. I subcontracted the job to a painter I knew and he was not professional. I put my trust into someone I knew and he walked away from the job, leaving me stranded to do

the work myself.

I quickly learned how to write up contracts and interview candidates for my jobs after that experience. Although I left that first painting job not satisfied with myself, I still learned from my mistakes. By 2016 things really started to pick up. I found a few guys I liked and they could paint. They had 10 plus years of professional painting experience. I also had gotten better at bidding jobs, which is a very important skill to possess in the construction industry.

The year of 2016 was filled with plenty of success for my business. We were offered contracts with the school system, Popeye's, multi-family units and residential homes. I didn't know that my business would grow so fast, but I wasn't complaining. Before the end of the year, my company went from a start-up to six figures. I am a firm believer in dreams coming true when you are determined to succeed. After putting so much time, energy and resources into my business I was happy to say I started a business in a field I knew little about and reached immediate success.

I wanted to share my story with you because my story does not differ from yours. If you are an aspiring or seasoned entrepreneur looking for an opportunity to succeed in your passion, then this message was meant for you. I have learned that the journey to success begins with a dream and the will to succeed. I never thought in a million years I would end up in construction, but fate sent that opportunity my way.

I went through many closed and opened doors before I saw the success I wanted as an entrepreneur. It doesn't matter where you are in life, where you grew up or what you have encountered. The only thing that matters most is what you are doing to become successful and reach your goals in this moment. I knew that entrepreneurship was for me because I was never happy in corporate America working in my field, even after going back to get my MBA. I knew that I deserved greater for myself and an extraordinary life was my destiny. Initially my journey was confusing because I did not understand where to start or where to go, but eventually things got better one day at a time.

Being a millennial entrepreneur can be challenging and just like all things there are pros and cons. I still wouldn't change this opportunity for the world. Growing my business from the bottom and learning every aspect of the company has changed me into a better negotiator, manager and businesswoman. I would like to encourage anyone who is interested in starting a business to start at the bottom of your company first. Don't start at the top of the chain where you have all the power to call the shots. Learn how to run the company from every angle, starting with understanding the products and services, managing the finances, balancing the books, marketing the brand, and increasing sales. Knowing this information will make you irreplaceable and untouchable.

I also want to encourage all entrepreneurs to embrace change and look forward to walking into new doors filled with new seasons and growth. Finally, follow your heart and never give up. When you finally realize the things for which you are passionate, the things that keep you awake at night, the things you will fight for, and the things you can't live without, then you have walked into a door of purpose.

Once you have realized those things and you are working towards them daily, then you have reached the place where you have fulfilled the desires of life. Always live your life. Be fearless, chase your dreams and walk into purpose. Don't let fear keep you from following your dreams, but instead let curiosity lead you to an abundance of success and prosperity.

ABOUT THE AUTHOR

Chisolu Isiadinso is a woman of integrity, passion, purpose, and vision. She is the Founder and CEO of Green Tiger Services, Inc. and Creative Director of *Chi the Prototype*.

When it comes to leadership, she understands the importance of leading, listening and learning. Having the opportunity of reigning as the 81st Miss Southern University A & M College has provided Chisolu with the tools needed to help and inspire others. During her reign, she was able to understand the importance of poise, perseverance, commitment, and dedication.

Chisolu works with both organizations and individuals. As a motivational speaker and one-on-one coach, Chisolu delivers results as she works with corporations, educational programs, entrepreneurs, schools, and universities. Chisolu's mission is to capture the attention of millennials and assist them with refining their purpose, so that they can become the ultimate prototype.

Chapter Two

Real Estate Dreams

By: Whitney Nicely

Millennials are in the best position of anyone in the history of time to become real estate investors. *Why?* We have access to deals across the country. We aren't limited to our own market anymore. With the power of the Internet, we can connect with friends online and share these opportunities with the masses, while easily finding new opportunities at our fingertips. It's so *easy* to start investing in real state but most millennials use the excuse that they don't have the money or the credit to get started. Think again.

I'm starting to think millennials don't buy houses because someone told them that they aren't *responsible* enough to own multiple houses yet...You don't have to wait your turn, guys. You can buy houses now. You *are* old enough. You *are* responsible, smart, courageous and brave enough to be a landlord. Buy more real estate *now*. Don't wait until you're older. I see some millennials running huge companies; other millennials are running all over the globe.

Trust me, real estate is within your reach. You're not a kid anymore, Millennial. It's go time! #millennialinvestor #ibuyhouses #letsgetrich

The Biggest Myth in Real Estate Investing

Millennials have been raised (or programed) to believe they need money and good credit to invest in real estate. It infuriates me, as a millennial real estate investor, because people don't need money nor credit to buy houses. Millennials were raised to follow the rules. Millennial parents were taught to follow the rules. Unfortunately, those "rules" being jammed down our throats without a second thought have been carefully crafted by another generation to keep us mentally acting like little kids for as long as possible or until we die.

Let me tell you how I buy houses without money, credit or banks.

This is going to shock you. You might call me a liar. You might shut this book right now and go on to think I'm somehow special or gifted and you might even think that the rednecks I work with in east Tennessee are crazy. I can assure you, this is not fake news. This is not a made-up story. Are you ready for it? I buy real estate with no money down. Credit is not a factor.

This is not a fly by night, get rich quick scheme that I made up. This is REAL real estate investing and bucking the system at every step. This is true grit and determination. This is my story as a millennial real estate investor.

My Inspiration

My mom bought a house from her brother in 1978 before she married my dad.

Lesson #1- She who owns the house, rules the house.

Hang on, though, my mom wasn't a loud, proud, bra-burning feminist. I never once heard her say anything along the lines of "Well, this is my house." She isn't the type to flaunt her investments. She merely goes about life; buying up the block and renting it back out in a gigantic game of "Who's got my money?"

My mom is also an introvert. Yes, my strong, determined, trailblazing momma is a quiet, homebody who surrounds herself with more family than friends. Her mother passed in childbirth when my mom was eleven. A workaholic father who had very little use for a a girl raised her. She learned to look inward for satisfaction rather than outward for support.

When my mom graduated high school, she went to work at the family's dump truck company. It was 1975 and she kept the same pay for almost 30 years. She is completely self-taught in matters of money, investing and running a small business. You see, my Pappaw was from a generation who thought girls were useless if they weren't in the kitchen, and they certainly had no business running the company operations.

My mom worked tirelessly with a smile on her face my entire life. Until 2003; my mom had a small meltdown. Without realizing it, this caused my little world to shift. My parents were fine; we aren't a divorce statistic. My mom simply decided she couldn't live on $19,000 a year anymore. After thirty years of devotion and consistency to the family's motto "Our bucks come from trucks," my mom hit a mental wall. It was weird to see my momma so brokenhearted.

I typically have a terrible memory but I vividly remember driving for dollars (even though I didn't know that's what we were officially doing until fifteen years later) with mom. She was crying and talking,

talking and venting, venting and scheming, scheming and crying. To say I grew up sheltered is an understatement. I had been with her every day for 18 years and I'd never seen my mom lose it until this one particular day.

Ever since I was a kid, I remember money showing up in the mailbox every single month. I thought everyone had people drop envelopes of cash in their mailbox at the first of the month. My brother and I used to race to the end of our driveway to get the checks out of the mailbox. I thought money just happened like that.

But in that moment in the car with my mom in early 2003, I realized money didn't just happen. My mom had saved every dime she could and then reinvested those pennies into houses so that people would send us money to live on every month.

My world came crashing down around me. My mom had fought for so long. And scraped together everything she could so I would grow up to believe money happened and life was whatever cake I wanted.

You know those moments in life where you get so mad at yourself for not seeing something that was so obvious and your eyes and your ears start to burn? Yeah. I was set to graduate high school in a few months and it was the first time that I realized that the world did not revolve around me. (Did I mention that I'm a stereotypical millennial sometimes?) I was furious. I hated my grandfather for the way he had kept my mom down for so long. That wasn't a big deal though because he didn't know my name. I hated myself for being such a nitwit and not realizing what my mom had gone through. And then, I'm ashamed to tell you for a few minutes (days) I was mad at my mom for taking it so long before she finally broke. What was wrong with her to let her dad, of all people, keep her from advancing in the company? Why couldn't she just step into a bigger role? Why didn't she demand more money? Didn't he have some duty to pay her more JUST for being his daughter? (See, that entitled millennial brain again?) I don't know why, but I told my mom to quit. She could get another job at another trucking company and instantly be more appreciated and better paid. I had no idea if that was true but that's how things happened in the movies so it had to be true, right? And God would provide for her, right?

Lesson #2- When it gets hard, don't quit.

Sow your seeds harder and faster. My mom explained to me that she barely graduated high school. She didn't have the same drive in her studies that I had. She didn't graduate in the top of her class. When she graduated high school in the 70s, people didn't go on to college unless they had a reason.

She explained to me that other trucking companies wouldn't want her because she couldn't type fast enough. She didn't have at least a Bachelor's degree in Logistics. She would have to start at the bottom but lower than where she was because the other companies were also family owned and she would be an outsider. Not only an outsider, but also she would basically be a Benedict Arnold for turning her back on HER family company and jumping ship to another company. She couldn't embarrass her family name, and told me quite frankly she wasn't a quitter.

Do you remember that moment in your life when your mom went from "Mother" to "Friend"? I don't remember the exact moment but it was March 2003, a few weeks after her breakdown. We were driving for dollars while I thought we were just practicing my driving skills.

By the end of March 2003, my mom had flushed the negative vibes out of her head. She had cried the last tear over her competency of running a small trucking business. She had planted her opinion and ideas into her brother's head and on her behalf, he convinced their dad to give her a shot at her own trucking company complete with a raise and a loan to get started.

Nicely's Construction & Excavating was founded 100% by my mom in April 2003. That's almost one month before I graduated from high school. Since I'm a millennial, I was a little perturbed she would try to steal my thunder from my own lifetime achievement (brat) instead of waiting until the Fall.

But this couldn't have happened at a better time for me. Looking back, this was at a time of my life that I was starting to really develop my brain while my mom was going through a growth spurt of her own. We were like two caged animals releasing our energy to the world. Of course, again, I only see this in 20/20 hindsight now.

At the time, I didn't realize how excited my mom was to see her trucks rolling up and down the interstate. I didn't appreciate my mom blossoming into her own life at the exact same time I was blossoming into my life. But I do remember thinking something amazing was happening to us at the same time. This is also where I started to realize how important it was that those envelopes of cash and checks kept showing up in mom's mailbox.

You Have to Invest in Something

One day, on a break from college life, I visited mom's new office that she had insisted be built. She was tired of being caged in a falling apart, duct taped together trailer and she set her mind to have a proper office built. It was gorgeous and HUGE compared to the

the tiny room I remember her being cramped in. I was there when she was counting and filling out the deposit slip for rent money.

"Mom, why don't I get mailbox money every month?", I asked.

This would have been a great time for my mom to go into teaching mode and explain cash flow, Monopoly, Robert Kiyosaki, banks, credit and other worldly things to my 21-year-old entitled millennial brain. But she didn't. She said as she laughed, "You have to invest in something."

That's it. No heart to heart fireside chat about the glories of real estate investing. Nothing about risk vs. reward. Just a quick, off-the-cuff, if you want it, go figure it out.

My mom might have raised one of the most entitled millennials you've ever met but she would also throw me out on my butt from time to time, too. Have you seen the YouTube video of the momma dog knocking her puppy down the steps to teach them about getting too close to the edge? That's a great illustration of how my mom taught me to invest.

She knew how to invest but she did it without a plan or a strategy. She knew real estate investing was totally doable but she had to figure it out along the way and apparently, she thought I needed a lesson in hard knocks instead of an "Easy" button. She had bootstrapped her way through life and it made her bigger, "badder" and stronger. She knew I had the same blood in me and I would figure it out.

Lesson #3- Figure it out... FAST.

Without a plan or real strong guidance, I decided that if she could figure out investing, so could I. Nearly SEVEN years and a lot of life lessons later, I got my chance to invest in real estate.

Imagine this... it's the first Saturday in December 2012 in Knoxville, Tennessee. I am 28 years old. I have been working at my mom's family trucking company since I got a bachelor's degree from UTK in 2007. I helped my mom and dad flip four houses over the past three years. I flipped furniture on Craigslist for extra money. I got a general contractor's license so the trucking company could get a job to develop a new roadway. I got a real estate license to represent my mom if she ever felt like buying a property from the MLS. I got an auctioneer's license so I could become a millionaire selling other people's farms quickly (or so I thought).

I was large and in charge, but I still didn't have mailbox money. I was on the hunt for a good deal... as long as it plopped down in my lap and had a bright red label on it that said "Buy Me Now."

The Four-Minute Leap

Part of the state's requirements to get a full-blown real estate auctioneer's license was to work under a broker and an auctioneer as an apprentice. So, the first Saturday morning of December 2012, I found myself at a real estate auction of 90 pieces of land that several local community banks were trying to offload as unpaid debts before the new year.

Yes, I was at a Foreclosure Auction. I was ecstatic to be there because I was killing two birds with one stone. I could help facilitate the paperwork for as many buyers as possible AND log the hours towards my auctioneer commitments! YES! If I got lucky, maybe

I'd meet someone trying to sell something and I could pick up a LISTING! Wahoo!

Then something weird happened. It started in my gut then quickly went to my brain, and before I could totally process it, the shift happened. We had 90 lots to auction. They were arranged in alphabetical order according to the county the land sat.

When the thought vomit started happening, we were on the "L" counties. People were bidding $500 or $1,000 per lot and the bank was accepting the bids on every one of them! Surely something is off, I thought. Is it legal to buy land for only $500 or $1,000 bucks? How much could it be worth?

I double-checked that my hearing and eyesight was clear with my broker who was sitting next to me at the back table.

"Are these people actually buying these properties for these prices or is this like a beginner price then it gets renegotiated later?" I blurted out.

She looked at me then realized I wasn't kidding. "No, Whitney. This isn't a trick. This is actually happening. Do you want to buy something?"

It hit me like a ton of bricks.

"Can I?!"

Now she was giggling, "Of course, you can buy something, silly girl."

By this time, we were into the "M" counties. One of the other apprentice auctioneers was scribbling down something in a note pad and BIDDING. I ran over to him and asked what he knew about the lots we were currently selling.

He said, "Buy the next one."

WHAT?! No dude, I just want the 411 on what's happening. I started to ask another question when the auctioneer started to rattle on the next lot.

"BUY IT GIRL!" Without thinking, I did what I was told to do by the other apprentice. I raised my hand. The auctioneer took my bid. Then someone else hit the bid. It was my turn to bid again.

"BUY IT GIRL!" I did it again. I raised my hand. The other person hit AGAIN.

By now, I felt like all eyes were on me. The auctioneer made a joke. The crowd laughed but I swear I only know that because people told me later how funny I looked throwing my hand in the air a third time and jumping when the auctioneer said "SOLD!"

Luckily, I was there that morning to work so the auctioneer just chuckled when he asked for my bidder number and I didn't have one. They just wrote my name next to my lot.

__MY LOT.__ Oh crap. What did I just buy? How much did I pay? Where was McMinn County? Isn't Decatur in Georgia?! Oh. My. Gosh... I didn't bring my checkbook! Would they take it away from me and rebid it because I was a silly little girl who came to an auction without researching the lots and bringing my freaking checkbook so I could actually PAY for the land I just agreed to take on?!

Thought vomit became word vomit in four minutes. Seriously y'all. In four minutes flat, I went from thinking "I should buy something today" to actually BUYING something.

People talk about the four-minute mile; I had the four-minute leap into investing. I didn't have time to think, research, plan, strategize or talk myself out of it. It was the most exhilarating four minutes of my life.

I was a real estate investor.

Instantly, I Was Hooked

As the day went on and the adrenaline rush started to slow down, my heart started beating regularly and I quit sweating like it was July... the answers started triggering in my head.

I had bid and won 1.07 acres in a failed subdivision in Decatur, TN. It was a buildable lot in a subdivision. Since there wasn't a house, I didn't have a street number. It was simply known as Rivergate Lot 12.

I had agreed to pay just over $1,000 for Rivergate Lot 12. Once the auctioneer's wife tallied my buyer's premium and taxes, the grand total for my four minutes of fun came to about $1,200. I was so excited I almost kissed her.

As soon as the auction was over, I raced down I-75 in the direction of McMinn County trying to beat the sunset so I could see my land. I wanted to touch the grass. I wanted to make it real in my head.

I'm very proud to let you know when I got to Rivergate #12, I was not disappointed in my purchase. It turns out that Rivergate is a fancy, gated subdivision with underground utilities, sidewalks, streetlights and a huge community-riding pin for horses. The horse field sits next to the neighborhood gazebo on the Tennessee River. Which leads the eyes to the boat launch and PRIVATE marina on the river.

I found out later that week at closing that the first 20 lots sold in the subdivision came with a deeded boat slip in the marina. And yes, that included Rivergate #12. I was a full-blown real estate investor! I had a chunk of east Tennessee dirt with my name attached to it.

The lady who had quit making payments to the bank on this land had originally agreed to pay $69,000 for it. I gave $1,200 bucks. Later on, after a bit of researching I found out that many of the lots had originally sold for $40k to $120k in CASH. The HOA restricted houses to be $250k or more in value.

I had unknowingly taken massive action and bought myself a genuinely solid return on investment as long as I could wait it out.

Four years later, I've only been to Decatur, Tennessee twice. Once the day of the auction and the second time the next weekend with my very proud mom, beaming dad and my totally confused boyfriend.

Lesson #4- Sometimes, the best exit strategy is to buy it and forget it.

That piece of dirt costs me about $100 a year in property taxes. Even though I don't drive by it on a regular basis, I know it's there. Even though it doesn't bring me heaps of money in the mailbox every month, it launched me into an exclusive club of real estate investors. It gave me the kick in the pants to buy more land. And then it gave me the confidence to start buying houses. Which led me to buy three apartment complexes. Who knew four minutes of blind courage on a Saturday morning could be the jumpstart to a lifetime of mailbox money from other investments?

Wait a second Whit…this property doesn't bring you any residual money, so why are you talking about mailbox money again? Well Grasshopper, six months after this auction I still had the taste of victory! I had been to several Saturday sales to gain exposure and log hours for my apprentice license since then. I also had a fire lit under my tail to flip more trucks and furniture than ever before. Except this time, I was nutting every penny instead of only saving half.

My mom had always bought her real estate properties with cash, so I decided to do the same thing. And in six weeks during the summer of 2013, I'd blown through my entire life savings. At the end of this whirlwind shopping spree I had bought; a half acre of industrial land in the city of Knoxville for $1,500 (I'll explain in a second), a flea infested, squishy-floored house on a bad street in a good neighborhood for $15k, someone's inheritance from a grandmother that ended up falling down a mountainside for $20k, and another inheritance down the street from where I lived for $30k.

My Hidden Treasure

Before we go too far down this quick spiral, let me tell you about that half acre of industrial land I bought. The first thing you need to know is there's a pyramid in real estate. Not a pyramid scheme but a hierarchy of land value.

Everything in America starts at the bottom as agricultural land, where crops and cattle are grown. The second tier of the real estate pyramid is residential land. This is where subdivisions, neighborhoods and regular houses are built. The third layer of the real estate pyramid is commercial land. This is where McDonald's, apartments and shopping malls are located. The tip top of the real estate pyramid is reserved for the most exclusive, the most desired, the highest taxed and the least restricted land use--industrial! It is used to hold factories, landfills and heavy-duty machinery. And I bought a half acre slice of it in the City of Knoxville for $1,500… all in, all done, all MINE.

The coolest part of this chunk of land didn't present itself until about three months after I had closed on it. I was downtown flirting with the county codes inspectors about another project when we started chit chatting about some of my investments. So, I told them about my little chunk of industrial land. They looked it up and found the hidden treasure I needed but had no idea existed.

It turns out that in 1992 (when I was 8 years old) there had been a road between my lot and my neighbor to the left. Since we were the only people who cared about this road, the city decided they didn't want to be responsible to keep it up anymore. So, they issued a Quit Claim deed giving the left side of the road to my neighbor... and giving the right side of the driveway to me!

The best part was my neighbor drove trucks back and forth all day every day on this driveway, thinking it was all theirs! I could hardly believe it so I ordered a survey to be conducted on the property lines and sure enough, it was true!

I was overconfident and marched my tail into my neighbor's office, completely ignoring protocol when one is dealing with a Fortune 500 company. I proudly told him those trucks were driving on *my* land and I expected to be compensated. Trying to hold in his laughter he said, "No, little real estate girl, that isn't possible." "Like hell it isn't possible. The city codes officers told me it was true and my surveyor confirmed it. Give me my money." He ushered me out of the office and told me he'd follow up.

Well, two weeks later I had a call from his secretary, "Ms. Nicely? We've recently had our lot on Prosser Road surveyed and we discovered that our trucks are driving on your side of the driveway. We'd like to rent that from you for $250 per month. Where should we send the check?" Ha! SCORE!

My momma didn't raise a fool though. Before I accepted the first offer, I asked if they would agree to maintain the property themselves and not call me if they needed a pothole filled or if a tree fell across the driveway. They agreed that was more than fair since they were the ones using the driveway to access to back of their building.

Then I asked if they would be willing to pay my property tax on the whole lot every year. It came to a grand total of $50 a year. The secretary giggled into the phone that they could handle that as well. Good. Write it up. I'll sign it. But one last request... See, I'd owned the property for about six months at this point, so I asked if she would pay back rent from the time I had purchased the property. Yes, they would be willing to send me a check for six month's rent at $250 per month and cover my property tax bill every year.

Without much prompting or planning, I got a check in the mail for $1,500. I had my whole investment back in Hip National Bank within six months of investing in this chunk of dirt and trees. I had negotiated a triple net lease on a property that will bring $250 a month into my bank account with **zero** overhead expenses for the rest of my life.

This is one of my favorite examples of how you can get started in real estate without much planning, over-analyzing or money. Deals like this one pop up all over the country every day but most people are so busy looking for that one out of the park homerun that they miss little dinky deals that could lead to a brighter future.

Now I also rent the main lot for $500 per month. Yes, I collect $750 per month on an initial $1,500 investment. How many times would you like to do that deal? Yeah, Millennial. You can do this!

I Went Broke Trying to Get Rich

But back to the summer of 2013, when I was buying more than I was renting… and certainly not on top of the mountain yet.

Somewhere in this buying spree of land and old houses, I ran out of money, brought my brother (and his life savings into the mix,) sold the flea house at a $4,000 loss and found myself a year after buying Rivergate #12 with a rented driveway on the industrial property, a rented house down the street from me and a never-ending money pit falling down a mountain. I had never been so happy in my life. I had put my money where my mouth was and in less than a year, I had mailbox money coming in every month just like my momma.

Lesson #5- Keep going.

Listen, Millennial. I've told you these little dinky stories about two little chunks of dirt on purpose. The media, the government and the good ole boys club of established investors has brainwashed you to think you need good credit, a LOT of money and experience to become a successful real estate investor. They've been lying to you to benefit their own game. The longer you keep your head in the sand, the richer they will become. Trust me on this fact.

The truth is what I've shown you. The truth is that these two pieces of Earth catapulted me into 57 creative financing deals in the past three years. As I write this chapter, I own 19 houses, 19 apartment units and 7 chunks of land across east Tennessee. I make enough passive income every month that I am able to help other newbie investors get started investing in real estate... without money, credit or experience.

You have the time, the skills, the drive and the ability to change your life, dear sweet Millennial. You can change the course of your family's life. You can stop renting, stop making someone else's mortgage payment, stop waiting until you're old enough, and stop dreaming. I'm 32 and I'm basically retired. Pension plans don't exist in our world. A 401(k) will never be able to keep up with inflation and our spending habits. The only chance you have to become financially free is to buy as much land as you can find. You have to start collecting rent instead of paying rent. You have to make a shift that you will live your life on your own terms.

You can do this, Millennial. I've done it and I know you can do it too. I went broke trying to get rich but you don't have to make the same mistakes. Let me know if you have any questions.

From one Millennial to another- I'm cheering for YOU. Happy investing!

ABOUT THE AUTHOR

Whitney Nicely went from no investments (or strategies) to 19 houses, 19 apartment units and 7 chunks of land in less than three years all bringing monthly money to her bank account on auto pilot.

She has travelled the United States speaking on stages, teaching her simple strategies, and meeting with other successful real estate investors, still buying houses the way she teaches others.

Whitney is a dog mom to Abby the Labby-130 pounds of loving fur, wifey to Jason East, an apartment investor, stepmom to Gavin (12) and Harrison (10).

Since 2016, Whitney has led and trained hundreds of future real estate rock stars to grow their portfolios, collect checks and achieve financial freedom. Hundreds of real estate newbies are securing leads, signing deals and scaling their dream incomes through the First Deal Done Fast Program.

Take the first step by joining Whitney's real estate investing Facebook group at WhitneyNicely.com/group

Chapter 3

Who Is Holding You Back?

By: Ashley King

As a child, if you were to ask me what I wanted to do when I grow up, my response would have been that I wanted to be an astronaut or to be rich. I was fascinated by outer space and all of its wonders. It's such a beautiful sight to see at night, and I wanted to be one of the few in the world to go into outer space. I also saw how money provided an opportunity to people. It seemed as if the more money you had, the better life would be. This was my opinion and my outlook as a child. I wouldn't understand until later in life what it would take to be rich, but at that time I just knew I wanted to have lots of money to buy the glittery and glamorous things I loved as a child.

My entrepreneur journey started in middle school when I began taking candy orders throughout the week from other kids. My father would take me to Sam's Club on Thursdays and Fridays to purchase candy in bulk to fulfill my orders. I would stand at the bus area dispensing the candy orders; I loved it. The fact that I could make money from an idea provided a rush and a thrill that I hadn't experienced before. I realized later that I got that determination and drive to make money from my father and my grandfather.

My grandfather and father were excellent examples of how hard work and dedication would pay off, especially financially. It wasn't until I was in my early twenties that I found out that my grandfather was a self-made millionaire. My grandfather didn't graduate from high school and perhaps not even middle school, but he was determined to make a living for himself and his family. I wanted that for myself and the family I would eventually have.

I was sitting in church one day when the pastor gave a testimony of a man with whom he had become acquainted. The man was a multi-millionaire with a lavish house, nice cars, and even a private jet. The pastor was describing the life and possessions that I wanted, so I was definitely on the edge of my seat listening intently. I can't recall what happened exactly, but it was a business deal that went wrong and caused the guy to lose everything he had.

All I could think about was the word 'everything': the house, the jet, all of the cars. I could not imagine the thought. How could someone lose millions? How could someone work so hard to build an amazing lifestyle and lose it all in the blink of an eye?

My heart was broken because the idea that I had that 'the more money I have, the better my future would be' was crushed. This story opened my eyes to the reality that money can come and go just like the wind. Money doesn't secure nor guarantee a better future.

The pastor continued with his story. I learned that although the guy had lost millions and he might have been down, he wasn't out for the count. The multi-millionaire had knowledge, drive and a skill set. That combination is more valuable than money. You may be wondering how valuable it may be? My answer to you would be 'priceless.' This is because with knowledge, the drive to meet goals and a particular skill set, this person (and anyone else in this situation) can make those millions once again.

After hearing this testimony it changed my perspective and my position on money. I was now old enough to understand that becoming rich doesn't happen overnight (even though TV and social media may have you to believe otherwise) and that just because you have money at a particular time, it doesn't always mean you would have money. It is more important to possess knowledge, drive and a skill set.

The pastor's sermon that day was an eye opener and led me down a different path. I no longer associated money with security. I reflected on my childhood days of how I just wanted to be rich. I began picturing the example of hard work from my grandfather and father, and I felt nostalgic when I thought back to middle school years selling candy. It dawned on me that it wasn't that I wanted to be 'rich', but that I wanted to be an entrepreneur. I wanted to create my own source of income, and control my destiny. I wanted the freedom.

I began to put a plan in motion and in time achieved my goals. Currently, I operate several businesses. I am a business strategist that specializes in helping working professionals launch their faith-based business (www.groomedforexcellency.com). I am also the founder of a nonprofit organization called CLASSIC (Christian Ladies Altogether Standing against Social Injustice Corporation). Also, I am the owner of a Christian apparel company called 1st Kings Apparel and the creator of the Live By Faith app. I am incredibly passionate about my faith and helping others; my life and my business reflect that. It is my ultimate goal to be an example of living a fulfilling life while serving God.

Obstacles

Of course, there have been obstacles. Just like life, in business there have been ups and there have been downs. As a millennial entrepreneur the list of obstacles that I have faced are numerous. However, many of them have been self-imposed. It was not my intent to stall my growth or block my success, but I inadvertently did so. I believe

that happens to many, especially when the dream and the goal are large.

Regardless of the generation, age or financial status, I believe all entrepreneurs have had a moment in which they may doubt or may have doubted if their dream would ever come to pass. My philosophy is that if your dream doesn't scare you then you aren't dreaming big enough, and my dreams are big. When setting out to achieve big goals the list to accomplish this dream can seem insurmountable. When starting a business, launching a product, and even just life, there are so many moving parts that are out of our control. This includes the economic condition, what other people do and what others think of you.

I learned early on that I could only focus on those things that I could control. Focusing on the things that are out of your control can leave you with a feeling of defeat and helplessness, both of which I started to know oh so well. When I began to feel defeated and helpless, I was hurting myself more than I realized. I began to have a victim's mindset. It was always someone else's fault and never mine. Having a victims' mindset cost me opportunities, hardship, and headaches.

Things became easier for me once I got rid of the victim's mindset. There are a few things that I had to learn which helped me reduce my stress and change my mindset that I'd like to share with you. I hope that you can learn from the things that I did or did not do initially.

1. Ask for help: I once was living and breathing insanity- day in and day out. Insanity is doing the same thing over and over again and expecting different results. I did so much all by myself and became frustrated that there was not the growth that I'd hoped to have. I decided to take control and try a different way. I had to take a step back and realize that maybe the way I was operating just was not working well for me. I then began to ask for help from others. I stopped being helpless and took action.

I had to take responsibility for my actions. In doing so it made me realize that no one can know it all. No one knows it all and asking for help didn't make me any less smart nor any less qualified. In fact, it displayed that I was smart enough to know that I couldn't continue doing what I was doing if I wanted to get different results. I stopped being "insane."

Many people continue to do the same things over and over in their businesses and wonder why there is no growth or sales. Something is wrong and you need to ask why? Why is no one buying? Could it be that the price is to high/low? Could it be the marketing or sales funnel? Could it be that honestly you don't know what you are doing? Or do you have a product that doesn't suit your target audience? There are plenty of people that can give you a fresh outside opinion and shed their expertise to help make your business better, but you have to be open, humble and ready to receive the help.

This brings me to my next topic. Once upon a time (and sometimes here and there) I lack…

2. Patience: I became incredibly humble and patient. I now know that success doesn't happen overnight. It takes hard work, long sleepless nights and plenty of sacrifices. You can't do what everyone else is doing and expect to be successful. If that were the case everyone would be successful.

For example, if someone wanted to lose weight, they are not naturally going to drop 40 pounds overnight. Sure, cosmetic surgery can aid in the process. However, those that undergo plastic surgery and those that lose the weight slowly the natural way, both must undergo lifestyle and eating changes to maintain their physique. It will take time to break those habits and maintain a new way of living. It takes time, energy and investment to have the right food, the right trainer, plan of action, etc. Nonetheless, it is necessary and essential for optimal health. It takes time to sustain lasting results.

The same principles apply to business. You can go the quick route and make up testimonials, buy likes and followers on social media to get clients, and give the image that you are qualified. However, if you don't know what you are doing, you are going to have some upset clients. Initially, you may get their money, but soon when people see that there is no value or lasting results in what you are offering, they will be screaming for a refund and calling you a scam.

Instead, you must put in the work consistently, and over time you will see the results. Slowly but surely when you invest your time and your energy, you will have the success that you want. Having patience and watching your business grow organically is much better than trying to take the fast route.

Proverbs 22:*1 states that a good name is more desirable than great riches; to be esteemed is better than silver or gold.*

Take your time and genuinely build your craft and expertise. If you truly bring people value and lasting results, they will refer you and your business will grow leaps and bounds. If you try to become an overnight success and defraud people of their money, people will speak negatively of you. One thing I can say about myself is that I may not have been patient, but I believed in being integral. I believe in grace and mercy, but you reap what you sow. What God has for is for you; do not rush it by trying to do too many things at once.

Looking at others on social media nowadays leads many to believe that if they are not doing twenty things at one time, then they are not effective. Have you ever met a person that does twenty things and does them all very well? As a wife, a business owner and all the other hats I wear, I entirely understand multitasking. However, I know that I cannot operate my business, do the laundry, clean the house, make dinner and meet a deadline all at the same time and do all of it well. I have lost count of the number of times I have burned a pot of rice, didn't give my best work or missed something obvious. It is possible to multitask, but don't put too much on your plate. Unless you have a team in place I recommend you start one thing and finish it before you start another, or at least be 70% complete before moving on.

Attempting to do many things and trying to learn so many things about your business at once will hinder you. If I were to scroll through my social media timeline I would find so many ads promoting things that I should be doing or should possess to grow my business. I have bought so many products that were supposed to help me build my business, but I haven't been able to even look at them all. What's the purpose of buying stuff to help me grow my business if I haven't even opened them? I had to overcome the pressure of feeling like if I didn't have the latest this, or if I weren't doing this, then I would be missing out.

The problem was that I was missing out on growth because I was wasting my money on things that I did not use. I was also wasting time reading and learning things that I had already learned. To prevent this, I suggest that you take an inventory of the things you already have so that you do not continue to purchase things that you do not need. Take inventory and also take the time to learn one subject at a time; don't overwhelm yourself with information. While you are learning, do not allow someone else's progress affect you. That's fine. Finish learning what you have and implement it.

Taking the time to write things down also helps me from becoming overwhelmed with information and things to do.

Habakkuk 2:2 states: *"Then the Lord replied: to write the vision; make it plain on tablets, so he may run who reads it."*

Simple meaning: write down your goals, make it understandable, and implement it. Many people hear this, but few adhere. I had a client that stated that she never seemed to have time to write her book. Understandably people have to work; they have their business, kids, etc. It's a matter of how productive you are with your time. She told me that she would plan her week for work. So I asked her why didn't she do that with her business and her life? Unless you have a clone that can handle your business, your life and work individually, then you need to create a plan for all aspects of your life and have a planner that sorts everything.

As a wife, business owner, employee, godmother, etc., I wear so many hats. I write everything in one place so that I can be as efficient as possible. I don't commit to doing a business event during the time of a weekend getaway with my husband. I don't promise a client something by a specific deadline if it's on the same timeframe as something that is due at work.

By having this all recorded in one place I can avoid double booking or overcommitting. For example, if I know that it will take twelve weeks of consistent promoting to efficiently build up momentum and ticket sales for my in-person event, then I'm not going to plan on promoting some other big project as I don't want to confuse my audience. Write down all your commitments and obligations in one place so that you will be productive and organized. One thing I forgot to mention that many people forget as well is to plan times in which you do something for yourself. Plan time to rest, to get a massage, to watch a movie. Plan something that's going to refresh you.

Less Comparison and More Collaboration: Another obstacle that I was able to overcome was feeling as though I had to compare and compete in order to be successful. The spirit of competition can be useful if you use it to push yourself, but it can be to your detriment if you use competition to compare yourself to others. Social media can either benefit you or break you if you allow it. Especially looking at all the selfies and happy pictures that people post. If you look at all the selfies and happy pictures that people post and compare it to your life, it could leave you depressed. It can have you thinking that everyone else's life is perfect and well put together, while your life is hanging on by a thread. Alternatively, you can be on social media connecting, building relationships, and learning from people.

At one time I would compare my growth and success with others, and it would leave me feeling inadequate. You have to realize that with social media, people get to pick and choose which aspects of their life they share. If I decide to do so, I can make my life look just as pretty and perfect on social media just like anyone else. I also learned that anyone could appear to be popular on social media, as people can pay for likes and subscriptions.

I stopped comparing myself and my business to others and started collaborating. It's amazing the opportunities that become available when you stop comparing and start working with other amazing people. Before I adopted the notion of collaboration, there was a person on social media of whom I was a little envious.

Before I began following her on social media, I met her at an event where I spoke and she was in the audience. At the end of the event she commented on how what I said helped her. We briefly kept in touch and she even attended one of my events. I followed her on social media, and over time I saw all her success and accomplishments. Over time I began to wish it were me. I knew she was not a social media fraud and that she was genuinely accomplishing her goals.

I never hoped anything bad for her; I was actually proud. But accompanied with being proud was the little green devil wishing it were me. He was hanging on my shoulder making me feel like I wasn't good enough as I kept comparing my life to hers. I loved what she was doing, but seeing it made me feel like crap. In the book "Grace Not Perfection" by Emily Ley, she quotes

Proverbs 4:23 *'Above all else, guard your heart, for everything you do flows from it.'*

She then goes on to state that especially online your heart needs to be guarded against those lurching feelings of inadequacy you feel when you look at people's profile or posts.

That resonated with me. I unfollowed the lady (but didn't unfriend her because she rocks!). I had to take away that thing that left me feeling envious and poorly about myself. It was nothing she did. It was a matter of guarding my heart. This is a valuable lesson if you have ever been on the other side of this; if people stopped talking to you or stopped following you on social media. As you can see, it is not always because of something that you have done to the other person. Many times it could be something going on internally with that person. You must just rock and the other person can't watch. The lesson: guard your heart and also don't take it personal if someone decides to guard his or her heart.

How have you been viewed as a millennial?

There are stereotypes placed on millennials. It is said that millennials are lazy, entitled, we tend that handle issues via text as opposed to face-to-face, that we are constantly job hunting and rely mostly on the Internet. I can't say that I fit into those stereotypes.

Generally, others say the exact opposite about me and are inspired by my hard work and tenacity. Many say that I am accomplished even though I feel like I am the type of person you will have to tell to sit down because I tend to do so much. Recently, my husband told me that he admires me because I set goals and go after them. Because of my efforts, I push him to go harder for his dreams.

It's amazing how people view me as such an amazing person. Some days I feel as though my efforts are in vain and I question whether or not I know what I am doing. To be honest, some days I am holding on by a thread, and if one more person asks me to do one more thing, I just may lose it! However, I continue to smile because I know that I am blessed to be in this position in life. I do not take my position nor my business lightly. People have placed their trust in me, and it's crucial for me to not only keep that trust intact but that I do so in the spirit of excellence. This is the rationale behind why I named my business strategist company 'Groomed for Excellency.' Outside of teaching working professionals how to launch their faith-based business, I let them know that it is a process to be outstanding. Rome wasn't built in a day, and the same holds true for a successful and sustainable business. Things take time.

There's a quote I recently heard by Michael Caine that I turn to when I feel overwhelmed: *"Be like a duck. Calm on the surface, but always paddling like the dickens beneath."*

However people may view you, you must know who you are. People's perception is reality. What someone perceives about you, whether good, bad, right or wrong, is their reality of you.

Why it was all worth it?

Entrepreneurship has taught me so much about myself. I have learned that:

- Hearing 'no' doesn't mean that it will never happen, but perhaps it's not the right time.

- Others may not see your vision, but they don't have your sight, so don't worry when other people don't believe in your dream.

- Feelings are not factual. We can lose a client and get upset. Someone buys a product and we get happy. Someone writes a bad review and we get angry. Emotions can be all over the place, but one thing that is constant and stable is God's love for me. So don't be swayed to make a decision based off of how you feel.

With entrepreneurship you have those long nights in which you need to meet deadlines, frustrating moments when you want to give up, and days where you are immune to coffee. But the moments when you hear that your book helped someone, how you inspired someone to launch their business or when your payment notification goes off (lol), those are the moments that make it all worth it. Entrepreneurship is messy and best suited for those who don't mind getting dirty. First, you have to build a solid foundation to have a lasting house. If your foundation is not right, then everything else will not stand the test of time. Many people want to bypass the building part and get right into making money. If the foundation of your house isn't correctly built then everything else added to it will eventually crumble.

Regardless of the obstacles that life or business may present, stay focused on your vision, don't become swayed by your emotions and don't rush the process. If you don't remember anything else, remember these two things:

- Faith without action is useless. No matter how much you hope and pray for your dreams to happen, if you take no action, nothing will happen.
- And let no one define and limit you. So many people define others by their past or limit you by their own beliefs. People change and rewrite history every day. It always seems impossible until it's done.

ABOUT THE AUTHOR

Ashley King is an entrepreneur's cheerleader. If you ever need someone in your corner, you would find her to be the loudest person in the cheering section. She inherited her mother's tenacity and her father's business savvy. Her ambition and faith is what drives her. The combination of all the above is why she is groomed for excellency.

A native of Atlanta, she is an author, Christian business strategist, founder of the nonprofit organization CLASSIC (Christian Ladies Altogether Standing Against Social Injustice Corporation), owner of a Christian apparel company 1st Kings Apparel and creator of the Live by Faith app. Her ultimate goal is to be an example of living a fulfilling life while serving God.

Chapter 4

Intuition Awaits

By: Christina Elkins-Thomas

Both of my parents were entrepreneurs. My father was a paralegal and my mother ran a daycare. So I got to witness first-hand what it was like to make money based on your own terms. There is something about creating a brand and actually closing a deal that's exhilarating. My first job was at my father's firm. He would often help non-profit organizations and small businesses filled their 501c3 and incorporation forms. He always jokes about how one of his assignments was to draw up a divorce. He got an A and used it to divorce my mother. I know it seems harsh, but they are both a lot happier now since they split. It was my job to organize the paperwork and file the different forms and articles. It's funny now, but back then we would save all of our files on disks and file them according to the client's needs. I learned so many things from working with him. At the time I had no idea what I wanted to be in life. But working with him taught me it was okay for me to dream even as an adult.

My mother was a stay at home mom during her second marriage. Occasionally things would get tight and she would open our house to other children. She has always been good with children; she turned it into a business. She took the necessary certifications to perform her job in excellence. After school, she had to pick up children. I still remember parents dropping their children off early in the morning. It's funny because she is a still friend with some of the families that she babysat for.

Working with her taught me that it's possible to find success in the least expected places. She also taught me that when doing business with people it is important to treat your clients and customers like family. People go into business in a specific industry strategically. I started selling body butters by accident. When I finished school, I found a job working at Cleveland Clinic, a hospital world renowned for groundbreaking research in open-heart surgery.

After about a year things looked scary. Our entire department was being phased out and there was nothing I could do about it. People were being written up right and left. I learned fairly quickly that nothing is guaranteed. I had been happy to find a job right out of college. But I was facing a level of uncertainty that made me uncomfortable. I began to think of creative ways to make money because I wanted to start my own business. I knew that I wanted to design something that would make people's lives easier. I began researching many different things.

In 2011, I invested in raw materials to make soap and other handmade personal care products. While in college, prior to working for the clinic, I moonlighted as a pharmacy technician. Working in the pharmacy allowed me to see creams and balms being compounded. These salves were for everything from eczema to diaper rash. I fell in love with natural remedies. In 2009 I went natural. My hair had been relaxed all of my life. The decision to go natural affected my life. Upon going natural I notice how expensive it was to purchase products. So I somehow created them in my kitchen. I was playing around with a few combinations of raw materials. One day I was walking through the kitchen and I noticed a batch of product on the table. Something told me to stop and investigate it. . I took the batch and used it for a twist out. My hair was so soft and manageable. The butter concoction worked better than anything that was available at the store. I also noticed that it worked wonders on my skin. Although the initial batch was an accident, I figured out how to recreate the concoction. My vision was to have a line of products. So I did my research and attempted to make other things. But to date, the whipped Shea butter is my number one seller.

Humble Beginnings:

I was so excited about my concoction I took it to work and shared it with my colleagues. One of my co-workers named Ms. Deborah was incredibly excited about it. She was so excited that she told her daughter and everyone in her department. People bombarded my cubicle asking for product. It got so bad she would come over every payday and buy two or three. One day she came over and told me that her daughter wanted me to bring some up to her job. I remember walking up the stairs in the hallway that led to her daughter's job. I was on my lunch break, so I was in a hurry. Her daughter was an administrator at a dentist's office. I prepared my products and placed them in a small box. When I arrived at the desk I asked for my coworker's daughter. "Are you the Shea butter lady?" she asked.

"Yes, it's nice to meet you," I said.

"Come on in," she said. She opened a door to the back of the doctor's office.

"You wanted the peppermint and the plain, right?" I asked.

"Yes, wait right here," she said, as she took her Shea butter and handed me money. She took me in the break room and introduced me to some of her coworkers.

"Are you the Shea butter lady?" they asked.

I said, "Yes." as they rummaged through the box. On my way out, a couple of the dentists came out of their exam rooms and smelled all of the scents I had. I walked out of the dentist's office with 120 dollars. That is when I knew that I had something special.

No Money: The Struggle is Real!

Once of the biggest struggles that aspiring entrepreneurs have is not having money. I have been around an entrepreneur or two. One thing that I find fascinating is hearing how they got started. I have done everything from business with family to doing business alone.

Every business is different and unique in its own way. When I started making products I had to sacrifice. Sometimes, I had no food for groceries. I had to budget to provide orders for people and live up to the demands. Once the product began to really sell, people came out of the woodworks looking for some. I didn't want to ruin my reputation so I had to put my money where my mouth was.

If you have a good product it will sell itself. Never give up, just because someone doesn't buy what you have right away, it doesn't mean they don't want it. I have learned that if it is something that they want, they will come back.

Some businesses have a low startup while others require funds. I have learned that it is best to keep my business money separate from my personal money.

Losing Focus:

Another struggle I have occasionally is losing focus. As a serial entrepreneur, there are always multiple things trying to grab my attention at once. As a result, I must put myself on a schedule for blogs, content, and products. Losing focus is detrimental to any business because it causes loss of time. To combat getting stuck in a rut I have to journal to see the vision of where I want to be. There are also times when frustration takes over. In these times it is especially important to journal. Journaling helps empty out the good and the bad to gain clarity to move forward.

Slow Seasons:

Everyone wants to have a booming business 24-7. Nonetheless, I have learned to appreciate the slow seasons. These times can be a struggle because it looks like nothing is working out. I found myself in another position after I left the first job; I was laid off. However, while working, I somehow found myself being the supplier of body butters. I can't lie, after what seemed to be the second layoff. I was discouraged and disenchanted with corporate America. Frankly, I was fed up and I had given up on the body butter business. I would be regular and live my life as an employee. Lo and behold I was in the cafeteria in the basement when I heard a familiar voice from the person behind me in line. "You got some of those butters?" she said.

"Ms. Deborah?" I asked as I looked at her familiar face.

"Yeah girl," she said before turning around and telling everyone waiting in line about the body butters.

It's funny because before I went downstairs, I prayed and asked God to reveal my purpose as it relates to his plan for my life. Somehow Ms. Deborah found her way back into my life. I was in what seemed to be a slow season. I had given up on my dreams and settled into being "regular" again. But when something is profound on the inside of you, The Universe…or what I consider God, has a way of reminding you of who you are.

Slow seasons are a part of the struggle that comes along with being an entrepreneur. As I used the slow seasons as an opportunity for preparation, more opportunities became available. And when the opportunities came I was more prepared to take them on. For me, there was always a lesson. Even when it seemed as though things were not making sense there was always something

Breaking the Stereotypes:

People have so many negative things to say about millennials. I think it's sad so many people believe all millennials are dumb, lazy and entitled. It is impossible to put us all in one category. In life, there are good people and bad people. One can't categorize the entire group based on the behavior of a few bad apples. However, I will address some of the stereotypes that people believe about millennials.

All Millennials are not lazy:

The first stereotype that came to mind is that all millennials are lazy. While there may be some that are lazy, we all aren't. I recently attended business seminar in which business funding was discussed. Some of the business owners believed that it's best to obtain a loan. Others argued that it was better to use your own money.

When I started my skincare business, I used my own money. This means I had to wake up every morning and punch a clock. I took the money from my job and invested in the materials I needed to make the butters. Remember that I have more than one business. Although I work a 40-hour a week job, I feel like I work two or three jobs because I am managing two other businesses and a non-profit. According to Waters, a study was done to determine the work ethic of millennials in the workplace. According to the study, "18-to-34-year-olds are working longer hours and taking less leave than any other age demographic," (Waters, 2017).

This means we aren't as lazy as they think. There is a lesson to be learned here. It is up to you to determine how you want to be defined. Don't live up to the stereotype no matter what people say. If you are an entrepreneur and you are good at what you do, don't allow negative narratives to stop you from achieving your dreams and goals.

There are so many things that exist now that make it easier for business owners. Back when I was working for and with my parents, things like social media and the Internet didn't exist. So I think that right now is a great time for business owners. But don't think that the Internet is your saving grace. I had to learn the hard way through various business ventures that word of mouth is everything. No matter how many followers and success you find online it is important for you to contact your local community for support.

Entitled or Nah?

One of my biggest pet peeves is hearing the stereotype that millennials think that they are entitled. Although this may be true for some, it is not true for all.

This is true as it relates to taking on new ventures in the entrepreneurial arena. We live in an era where information is accessible. For years corporate giants have been privy to proprietary information as it relates to technology and vendors. The Internet has made it possible for almost anyone to open a business. With enough dedication and research, the sky is the limit.

Many corporate giants are falling fast and hard. People are turning to the internet and independent merchants to get what they want. This means that business as we know it has changed. Corporate giants like Wal-Mart are revisiting non-conventional business practices to stay competitive with companies like Amazon. Recently they offered site to store pickup and outside vendors.

There here has been a paradigm shift in business, as we know it. Regular people can sell whatever they want! Companies are turning to influencers to drive traffic and awareness to their businesses. This is an excellent time to be in business. Perhaps for those millennials that work hard, entitlement looks like opportunity. Perhaps millennials have it somewhat easier because technology has given this generation an unfair advantage. Fortunately, nothing replaces hard work. Even with the advantages and technological advances, one must have a certain level of persistence to survive.

Some see social media and technology as an advantage. However, it can also be a burden. Millennials and those who were born after must face a new set of challenges. Social pressure is different because people must be authentic in an age where authenticity is scarce. Our generation is constantly bombarded with images and information. We must try to process our own desires and aspirations without becoming lost. Many millennials are perceived as entitled when actually we are simply seeking new opportunities to recreate and reinvent ourselves. Information that seems innovative is somewhat common knowledge because we must adapt quickly to stay ahead of trends.

We have brains too:

The last stereotype I will share and debunk is the notion that millennials are not smart. I have heard so many news stories and comments about our generation needing Google to survive. The cool thing about being a millennial is that I can still remember doing my homework using the Britannica Encyclopedia. There are many millennials that do not value knowledge. The small percentage that do, have a heavy load to carry.

In order to remain competitive from a global standpoint we all must step up and be the best version of ourselves. From a business standpoint, I have experienced situations in which people have treated me

As if I were dumb. I am the type of person that will just sit back and read a situation before I become involved. The sad part is that both millennials and baby boomers have treated me this way.

People like to judge you before they get to get to know you. It doesn't bother me. People in society like to make it seem like a person should be defined by their occupation. When people treat me this way I just see it as an opportunity to show them they are wrong. Success speaks louder than any argument. While most people that are my age are out partying, I am writing, reading and learning. Nothing worth having will come easy so I continue to prepare myself for the future.

Mindset:

Mindset is imperative for anyone who wants to achieve anything worthwhile. We can only achieve what we believe. It is true. When I got my undergraduate degree, I applied for a position I had received training for. Coming out of school I had been trained to be a technical writer. I was so excited and adamant about getting a technical writing position. I applied for every position I could find. Shortly thereafter I landed an interview in downtown Cleveland. I live in Cleveland and downtown is a big deal.

Cleveland is a semi-Midwestern city with a New York vibe. I was born in Houston, Texas and moved up to Cleveland shortly after I completed high school. So for me having a job in a big city working downtown is like having one dream come true.

I got to the interview and clammed up. I didn't have the confidence to try to sell myself. I didn't get the job. For years I did not apply for any other positions. I allowed fear and anxiety to keep me stuck in jobs I in which I knew I was overqualified.

The lesson I learned from this whole scenario is that you have to believe in yourself even when no one else does. Don't allow fear and anxiety to cause you to miss out on opportunities. My goals have changed. I'm not that afraid little girl anymore. I am now a woman with a vision. I am a woman with a business. My goal now is to secure the bag and eventually rent out some space and open a store downtown or anywhere in Cleveland. Your entire life changes when you change your mindset and make up your mind that you want success.

Negativity:

Don't allow others to define you. I was on Instagram the other day and I saw a video of Oprah. A reporter was interviewing her. He asked her about her new show. He asked her what she would do if things didn't work out. I loved her answer and the confidence she exuded when she answered. The answer she provided was not nearly as important as the peace she had when she answered.

On the journey of entrepreneurship, I have seen my fair share of negativity. There are two levels of negativity. There is the negativity that comes from other people. Then there is the negativity that comes from within. I had to learn early on the surround myself with people that supported my dreams. One way to eliminate the negativity that comes from others is to eliminate the people that bring the negativity. I have learned there are times when the journey takes you to places where everyone can't go. I never understood that until I saw more doors open.

The opinions of others are not as important as your own opinion. The biggest mindset challenge I have had to overcome is talking myself out of it. Journaling has helped me tremendously. You don't know where the journey will take you. Over time I have learned the importance of not giving up. I'm grateful to have people that believe in my products enough to push me. Now I am at the point where I must believe in the brand even when no one else does.

As a child my parents instilled in me importance of words. You will have what you say. Be very careful about how you speak about your business. Whenever I have feelings of negativity I speak what I want to see instead of what I see. You can only go as far as you believe.

Tunnel vision:

There are so many distractions; especially with technology. Social media can be a major distraction but it need not be. I find that content planning helps save time. Hours of scrolling equate to hours of missing out on achieving goals and dreams. I had to learn the hard way how to have tunnel vision.

Without tunnel vision, I always end up in a place of regret. For example, whenever I waste all of my time procrastinating, I miss out on money! I have lost out big time because I hesitated or got side-tracked. So I try to have a set schedule for each thing that I need to tackle.

I have learned to delegate certain days of the week for specific tasks. By establishing a healthy routine, I can get more done. Doing tasks in small increments helps me save time eventually. It also helps me maintain my focus. It is better to have laser beam focus on one thing than to have a little focus on many things.

Marathon:

When I started my business, it was difficult for me to see past what was in front of me. I would fulfill the orders and preorders and then get kind of stuck occasionally. After a few years, I saw that it is important to plan for the future. To find success in business one must plan and endure for the long run. When I treated my business like a short-term venture, I found short-term results. However, when I treated my business like a long-term vision, I endured the obstacles and trials that come along with being an entrepreneur. Having a marathon mentality gives me the ability to withstand discouragement, discontentment, and fatigue.

People do not just wake up one day and decide that they want to run a marathon. Planning and practice are vital. They are a part of a process that gives you the ability to run the race. Have clear goals and objectives. Having a marathon mentality helps me set realistic goals.

I am happy to be a millennial in business. It is both an honor and a privilege to build a legacy for my family. There are so many elements in business that give an advantage. However, I must put in the work to get where I am going. People often overlook, profile and undermine my abilities as a minority millennial in business. But I am determined to take the negatives and turn them into an opportunity to make money. Over the years I have learned there will be struggles and stereotypes, but having a strong mindset is crucial.

If you are reading this as a millennial I want to encourage you. You have the power to be everything that you want to be. Pay attention to the signs around you and live your truth. Go with what works. If you have an idea or a business stick with it until you see progress. As a serial entrepreneur I have experienced setbacks, self-sabotage and failures. I will not make it seem as though starting a business is easy because it is not. Sometimes I have wanted to give up. There have also been times where I have had to work a 40-hour workweek to support my dream, only to come home and keep working until 1 am in the morning. It is difficult. The sooner you get serious about your business the sooner you will make money.

About The Author

Christina Elkins-Thomas is a Marketing strategist, Co-author, and serial entrepreneur. When she isn't writing, she creates websites, commercials, and strategies for SEO, Social Media, and Website Analytics. Although she was once homeless, she has gone from being labeled as hopeless, to finding hope and becoming an entrepreneur. She attributes all of her victories to her personal relationship with God. She is a wife and the mother of two boys. In her free time, she enjoys listening to music and writing. She has also founded Chrissy Scents which is a natural skincare line.